*Aussie Heroes*

# DAME NELLIE MELBA

Written by Gabiann Marin   Illustrated by Rae Dale

With historical advice from Sue Thompson
- curator of the Nellie Melba Virtual Museum

To my Mum - my personal Aussie Hero

## GM

First published in Australia in 2010
by New Frontier Publishing
Suite 3, Level 2, 18 Aquatic Drive
Frenchs Forest nsw 2086, Australia
www.newfrontier.com.au

National Library of Australia Cataloguing-in-Publication entry
Author: Marin, Gabiann.
Title: Dame Nellie Melba / Gabiann Marin ; Rae Dale.
Edition: 1st ed.
ISBN: 9781921042645 (pbk.)
Series: Marin, Gabiann Aussie hereos.
Target Audience: For primary school age.

Subjects:
Melba, Nellie, Dame, 1861-1931--Juvenile literature.
Sopranos (Singers)--Australia--Biography--Juvenile literature.
Women singers--Australia--Biography--Juvenile literature.
Opera--Biography--Juvenile literature.

Other Authors/Contributors: Dale, Rae, 1945-

Designed by Nicholas Pike

Dewey Number: 782.1092

Printed in China

# Contents

# Chapter One
# Young Diva

Six-year-old Nellie crouched up in the tree branches, peering down at her father as he approached the dam. She knew she would be in trouble if he found her sitting in the old gum tree, sopping wet, so she decided the best thing was to stay very quiet until he passed.

Suddenly, her father looked up into the tree, straight at Nellie. She shrank back against the smooth bark, but she knew it was too late, she'd been spotted. At that moment, she heard the humming, a favourite song of hers that her mother used to sing when she was a baby. After a moment of listening, Nellie realised the humming sounds were coming from her! No wonder her father had seen her, the sounds of the song had alerted him. Nellie mentally willed herself to stop humming the tune and then, as her father glared at her, she clambered down onto the grass below. She smiled at him, hoping to win him over. Although her father was gruff in his proud Scottish way, she knew he had a particular soft spot for her, even if she was a bit of a tomboy.

'Your ma has been calling you for well over an hour,' he said sternly.

Nellie bit her lip and looked down at the ground.

'Have you been swimming in that river again?' her father asked.

Nellie shook her head. 'No Father.' She looked at her dripping dress, then peered up trying to look contrite. 'I just fell in, but I got out right away.'

Nellie's father shook his head. He knew his daughter was lying, but he didn't really mind. As much as he would never admit it, he loved Nellie's spirit.

'Your grandmother is waiting for you. Have you forgotten ?'

Nellie's eyes lit up. She had forgotten. Today, she was to make her very first appearance singing in public. Her grandmother had arranged it as a fundraiser for the local schools. Her mother and father weren't sure about her singing in public, but her grandmother had insisted, saying that everyone in Richmond had heard of the little girl with the voice like an angel, and would be clambering to see her. It was an excellent opportunity to raise money for the school and introduce the gifted girl to society.

Nellie's father didn't think she looked much like an angel at that moment, more like a drowned rat, but he had to agree with his mother-in-law, Nellie's singing voice was quite exceptional.

'Come on then, get a hurry on, or your

mother may forbid you from going,' he said, striding ahead.

'I'm sorry, father,' she said, 'let's hurry.' Nellie hiked up her skirts and began to run ahead, forgetting her father's annoyed mood in her rush to get home and into her recital dress.

'Helen!' her father called. Nellie stopped in her tracks, knowing better than to push her father once he used her full name. 'Ladies do not run in that manner. Have a little decorum, please.'

Nellie nodded, and slowed her pace to

a hurried walk, which her father easily matched with his long, forceful strides.

'Stop that infernal humming,' he said.

Her mother, Isabella, was seated with Nellie's grandmother. When Nellie rushed into the drawing room, her mother grimaced at her appearance. Nellie's dress and pinafore was caked with mud and her hands were grimy. The ribbon was long gone from her hair, which was wet and unkempt.

'For heaven's sake, Nellie, go and change into something dry,' her mother said.

'Sorry Mother. Hello Grandmama,' Nellie said, beaming at her beloved grandmother.

'Oh Nellie, don't you look a fright.' But her grandmother was smiling sweetly. Nothing Nellie did seemed to bother her at all.

Nellie dashed off, and returned with her hair brushed and wearing a new, clean dress. 'I'm ready,' she announced, waiting expectantly by the door.

Nellie's grandmother got up and took her granddaughter's hand, leading her out to the awaiting carriage. 'Have you practiced what you are going to sing, Nellie?'

'Yes Grandmama, *Comin' thro' the Rye* and *Shells of Ocean.*'

Grandma grinned. She had taught Nellie those songs and knew the girl would sing them beautifully. 'Very good. Let's get off then.'

Nellie's father and mother followed Nellie into the carriage, seating themselves opposite her and her grandmother. Isabella was holding Nellie's four-year-old sister, Anne, in her lap. Everyone was excited, but no-one spoke the whole way. Nellie, quite wisely, was saving her voice.

The Richmond town hall was not as crowded as Nellie had been hoping, but her grandmother assured her it was a good turn out, and that she should give it all she could.

'This will be the first of many audiences for you, Nellie,' she said. 'You must do your very best every time, for once they love you, you'll never want to disappoint them.'

Clambering onto the rough stage, Nellie noticed the hall was quite full and that many people in the back of the audience had to crane their necks to see her on the stage. She thought for a moment, then went to the back of the stage and retrieved a chair which she stood upon, making her easily seen by the people in the back rows. There was an expectant hush, then Nellie began to sing.

'My,' her mother remarked to her father sitting in the audience, 'she really is very good at this.'

Isabella was not truly surprised by her daughter's abilities, as Nellie had been singing since she could talk, and loved to be surrounded by music of all types. Nellie's musical ability was the one thing that Isabella hoped would make her tomboyish, forthright, little girl suitable for polite company.

Everyone in the hall was rapt by the beautiful sound of Nellie's singing. By the end of the piece, everyone applauded her. Nellie grinned; it was her first performance in front of an audience and, just as would be the case in the future, she was the star of the show.

'Nellie sings like an angel,' her grandmother stated as they left the hall. Nellie blushed, pleased she was getting such great attention from her family.

'She should be on the stage professionally,' Nellie's grandmother continued. Nellie's mother shook her head. 'No, no, Nellie is not interested in any of that sort of thing. Her singing is lovely, but no polite girl would ever wish to make a name for herself on the vulgar stage.'

But Nellie was interested in that sort of thing. In fact, it was what she wanted more than anything else in the entire world. Every night she dreamed of being on the stage with a crowd of beautifully dressed people applauding her, and every morning she wondered how she could make her dream come true.

However, the stage and the applauding crowds seemed a long way off as Nellie sat with her mother the next day doing needlework. Nellie hated needlework and embroidery, and would have preferred to be running around outside like the boys in the neighbourhood did.

'Could we play something on the piano, Mother?' she asked.

'No Nellie, your needlework is appalling, you need to practice.'

Nellie slumped in her seat and started to hum one of her favourite songs by a composer called Mozart.

Isabella looked over at Nellie irritably. 'Nellie, please. Just be quiet and finish your embroidery.'

'Embroidery is boring.'

'Nellie!'

'Well, it is.'

'All ladies must know how to embroider, Nellie. Your stitch work is terrible. You'll never get married with stitches like that.'

'I don't care to ever get married,' she replied.

Nellie's mother tried to hide her shock. It was expected that every girl would get married and, therefore, it was assumed that getting ready for marriage was the most important thing in every girl's life.

'Nellie, all young ladies want to get married and have children and be good wives,' her mother said.

'I don't. I want to be on stage and sing.'

Nellie's mother sighed, thankful at least that Nellie's father had not heard that particular comment from his daughter. After all, he would be most displeased.

But Nellie's father, David Mitchell, was never really displeased with Nellie. In fact, he was secretly proud and amazed by his young daughter and her determined ways. He was a wealthy and influential man in Melbourne, something he believed he had earned through hard work and determination. David Mitchell was far from a soft man, but, as Nellie suspected, he did have a soft spot for her. He saw a lot of himself in her stubbornness and although he knew that Nellie would not be accepted into polite Melbourne society unless she became more lady like, he would often encourage her adventurous ways, taking her out on bushwalks or riding with him. The times she spent with her father were some of the happiest – yet most confusing – times of Nellie's life.

For example, once when they were out riding, the wind blew her hat off and she was forced to stop and dismount to retrieve it. Instead of waiting for her, as she had expected, her father rode on, expecting Nellie to catch up, which she did, breathless and flustered.

'Why didn't you wait?' she cried, annoyed with him.

'You are going to make us late now,' was all he said, and galloped on.

From that day forward, Nellie understood that her father would never make allowances for girlish behaviour, at least not in his daughter. In her father, she had a strong ally, but also a fierce judge of her behaviour.

# Chapter Two
# Away from Home

'Are you sure it's the right decision?' Nellie's father asked, as he watched his wife instruct the maid to pack Nellie's bags.

Isabella turned and nodded. 'She needs to learn how to be a proper lady, otherwise we will never find a suitable match for her.'

Nellie's father reluctantly agreed, but still it was hard for him to send his headstrong, vexing daughter away.

'Can I sit up with the driver?' Nellie asked, as her mother led her towards the carriage.

'No Nellie, it's not proper. You should sit inside the carriage with us.'

'But you can't see anything from in there,' she complained. Nellie's father picked her up and loaded her on the front of the carriage next to the driver. Nellie's mother gave him a despairing look, but said nothing as she got into the cab and settled herself in.

'Thank you, Daddy,' Nellie said, adjusting herself into the seat and securing her hat. 'Now I'll be able to see any black snakes on the road and stop the horses being bitten.'

So Nellie arrived at her new ladies boarding school with her hair and hat blown about in a frightful manner. Her embarrassed mother tried as best she could to smooth her hair to make her daughter look presentable.

At school, Nellie was miserable. She had to act as a lady at all times; something that was very hard for her to do. Plus, music was not a focus at boarding school the way it had been in Nellie's home, and she missed it terribly.

Meanwhile, the teacher's had spotted Nellie as potential trouble the moment she had arrived, windblown and bouncy. They were determined to break her spirit and watched her constantly, harping on every small mistake she made.

'I can't stand it here,' Nellie told one of the few girls she had befriended. 'I'm getting out.'

'How?' her friend asked.

'I don't know yet, but I will. They can't keep me cooped up in here like a prisoner.' Nellie snuck away from the teacher's gaze every chance she got. Hiding under the buildings and in broom cupboards, and sometimes getting into the teacher's staff areas, Nellie would happily sit and sing to herself until she was eventually found.

Although she wasn't actually free from the school, at least she could avoid the constant stares and punishments of the teachers for a few hours. The misery of being caned, and the discomfort of writing lines and lines of words on the blackboard never quite erased the moments of freedom she had experienced.

Then one weekend, when they were supposed to be in their dormitories reading or revising their lessons for the next week, Nellie and two friends snuck out of the school grounds and hitched a ride on a farmer's cart into the city.

Nellie loved the city of Melbourne. The crowd of people rushing about was frightening, but also exciting. Best of all, there seemed to be music everywhere - the clopping of horses, the stamping of feet on the pavement – which was in great contrast to the enforced, sterile silence of the school.

'Hey look over there,' one of her friends said, pointing to a strangely dressed woman sitting at a table in the park. 'What do you think she's doing?'

Nellie shrugged her shoulders. She didn't know, but whatever it was, it looked interesting. The woman looked up as the girls approached, and Nellie sat down on the chair opposite her.

'What are you doing here?' Nellie asked.

'For tuppence I can tell your fortune,' the woman replied.

Nellie plucked a coin from her purse and handed it to the woman, 'And what will my fortune be?'

The woman gazed at Nellie for a few moments then nodded. 'You are going to be a great singer. You will travel the world, but you will always have the place you were born with you. You will die here, but after a long and amazing life.'

Nellie sat back, a little surprised. The other girls chattered excitedly. Nellie stood up, hiding her emotions, fearful to believe that the one thing she wanted more than anything could actually come true.

'We better get back before bed check,' she said, turning and walking away from the fortune teller. As the girls walked towards Market Street, Nellie turned back to see the woman one last time, but she was gone.

# Chapter Three
# Tragedy Strikes

Nellie finished school at the end of the year in December 1880 having turned nineteen in May of that year.

She was a headstrong teenager, eager to leave school and start her real life, which she was sure was going to be much more exciting and adventurous than the dreary years she'd spent at school. Graduating with average grades, she returned home to her family, which had grown to seven siblings, including her youngest sister, four-year-old Vere, who she quickly came to adore.

Although she was now older and better educated, Nellie was far from the refined, polite, softly spoken lady that her mother had hoped she would become. Instead, she was wilful and opinionated. She still enjoyed the outdoors and spent many hours with her father, riding around the property and walking in the bushland, just as they had when she was a child.

The other thing that had not changed was Nellie's love of music. She had signed up for singing lessons with famed Italian opera singer and teacher, Pietro Cecchi. She spent hours with Cecchi, singing scales and learning the strange Italian words that were the basis of most of the great operas.

Perhaps because he resented his daughter's strong friendship with Cecchi, Nellie's father strongly disapproved of her time with him and objected when she voiced ambitions to sing on the Melbourne stage. It was her mother, this time, who ensured that Nellie could keep singing.

'David, you know that when Nellie sings she is happy, and when she is happy she is more amiable. No man will want to marry an unhappy, miserable woman,' her mother argued.

'You spoil her, Isabella. Where will it all stop? You know she has plans to debut her singing publicly in Melbourne in a few months.'

'So let her. It will be forgotten very quickly when she marries and has children. Right now, it may be the only thing she can do which will attract a man of any standing. Remember, one of the things that attracted you to me was my piano playing.'

So Nellie's father permitted the lessons, and Nellie started to plan for her big singing debut in the town hall. It seemed the fortune teller in the park was right after all; Nellie was destined to become a great singer.

Nellie practiced and practiced, every day her voice getting stronger.

One afternoon, she returned home, excited about her singing, only to find her father and her sisters and brothers sitting silently in the living room. Her youngest sister, Vere, was being held tightly in her father's arms.

'What's wrong?' Nellie asked, her good mood immediately disappearing.

'Mother's gotten worse,' replied Nellie's sister, Anne. Nellie looked over at her father, but he would not meet her eyes. Isabella had been ill for months, but everyone had acted as though it was a small set back, and that she would soon be well again. The idea of her mother not getting better came as a shock.

Nellie raced up the stairs to her mother's bedroom and flung the door open wide.
She expected to see her beautiful mother sitting in the chair by the window doing her embroidery, as she often did. But she was not sitting in the sunshine of the window. In

fact, the room was dark, the shutters drawn tight, and in the dimness, Nellie's mother lay on the bed.

She looked over as Nellie barged in, and smiled weakly. That was her Nellie, always rushing about, always so energetic and full of life.

'Nellie,' her mother whispered. Nellie rushed by her bedside. 'Nellie, you must look after Vere. She is too small to lose her mother, you must help her.'

'Don't be silly, Mother,' Nellie chided, 'You'll be up and around in no time.'

Nellie's mother shook her head and gestured for her daughter to be quiet. 'You know Vere has never been strong, not like you Nellie. You were strong when you were born, you will always be strong. She'll need your strength.'

Nellie wanted to interrupt, to tell her mother that Vere was fine, that they would all be going to her professional debut. But Nellie's mother would not allow her daughter to speak, except to promise that she would care for her youngest sister. Nellie nodded. 'Of course. Of course, I will,' she promised.

Nellie's mother smiled, then gestured to Nellie to leave the room. 'I need to rest my eyes for a moment, Nellie.'

Nellie left, closing the door quietly behind her. She went down to the drawing room where her sisters, brothers and father sat, silently. She took Vere from her father's lap and hugged her close.

Nellie's mother died a few days later and, true to her promise, Nellie insisted on treating Vere as though the child was her own, moving her little sister's cot into her bedroom and fussing over her. She took Vere to rehearsals and to the park, everyone commenting on how fragile and delicate the little girl was; such a contrast to her elder sister.

Nellie checked on Vere constantly, noting every sniffle and cough. When, one night, she noticed her sister was very ill, she begged her father to get a local doctor.

Her father shrugged it off and said dismissively, 'Vere is always sniffling.'

Nellie was not convinced, but she finally went to bed, still worried about her sister. Late that night, she was awoken by a noise in her room and looking around in the dark, she saw a white figure bending over Vere's cot. Spooked, Nellie got up and saw that the figure was her mother, pale and ghostly. She stood, terrified, as her mother's ghost turned to her and pointed down at Vere, then vanished. The next morning Nellie told her father of the strange incident.

'Tut, tut, girl,' he said, disappointed that his usually practical and clear-headed daughter could entertain such silly fancies. 'Get those foolish notions out of your head.'

'Please father, at least send for a doctor. You know Vere is not well.'

Nellie's father considered this for a moment. 'I will get a doctor when I get home this evening. Will that satisfy you?'

Nellie agreed reluctantly, and left the room

to check on her baby sister, pleased that a doctor would soon be called. But before her father organised the doctor's visit, little Vere passed away.

Nellie was beside herself with grief: first her mother and now her precious baby sister. All thoughts of singing, even of her grand Melbourne debut, were forgotten.

The Mitchell family was lost in its grief for several months. No-one spoke of the future. The children just got through the days, looking after their grief-stricken father.

Nellie felt terrible, but couldn't help thinking that this enforced isolation after the deaths of her mother and sister were not going to do any of them any good. So she encouraged her father to take a job he had been offered in Mackay, Queensland, to organise a new building project.

Her father resisted the idea at first, but even he had to agree that a fresh start for the family would probably be a good thing for them all, so he arranged for Nellie, Anne and himself to relocate to the northern Queensland town to take up the new opportunity.

Nellie worried about leaving her beloved Melbourne, but went without complaint, looking forward to the brightness of the Queensland sun after enduring months of the wet Melbourne winter.

# Chapter Four
# Stuck in the Outback

Nellie found the friendliness and sunshine of Mackay a great tonic to her grief, and she and Anne soon established themselves as the belles of the town. They attended tea parties and boating expeditions, plus there was plenty of bushland for Nellie to explore on horseback.

Even her father began to blossom in the Queensland sun, often accompanying Nellie on her outings and attending many of her popular singing recitals, which were organised by the people of Mackay when they realised they had talent in their midst.

While Nellie was happy to see her father enjoying his life a little more, she couldn't help but notice his possessiveness over her. He was particularly protective when gentlemen callers requested that she accompany them to plays or concerts.

Nellie felt resentful at his continual refusals to let her see anyone seriously. Anne, however, never failed to stick up for their father.

'He just wants what is best for you, Nellie,' her sister would say when Nellie complained of another suitor being turned away.

Nellie couldn't help noticing that their father paid far less attention to who was courting Anne. Although, she supposed that because Anne was only popular because of the reflected glory of Nellie herself, there were fewer suitors to turn away.

Still, Nellie had her recitals and social events to keep her happy, and the truth was that there were no gentlemen in Mackay to whom Nellie felt any particular attraction. Not, that is, until a young man named Charlie Armstrong rode into town.

A dashing young man, distantly related to British nobility, Charlie had travelled widely and had lived in London, making him a much sought-after guest at all the best dinner parties in town. It was not his breeding, however, that attracted him to Nellie, it was his taste for adventure. He worked as a jackeroo on outlying farms, and entertained dinner party guests for hours by regaling them with stories of the bush and of his encounters with snakes and breaking in wild horses called brumbies.

Nellie and Charles soon became constant companions on the Mackay social scene, with most of the townsfolk accepting that the noble jackeroo and the gifted singer made an excellent match. Everyone, except Nellie's father.

'Are you coming to my performance, Father,' Nellie asked at dinner the night before one of her recitals.

'I am too busy for such trivialities, Nellie,' he replied.

Anne, sitting across from Nellie, saw her sister's face fall. As much as Nellie may protest that she didn't care what her father thought, they all knew that Nellie craved her father's approval more than anyone else's.

'Well, no doubt you'll read all the wonderful reviews in the paper on Monday,' Nellie said, covering her disappointment.

Nellie's father said nothing and got up from the table, excusing himself. 'Charles will be there, so I will have a ride home,' she added.

Her father stood stock still, then spoke without turning towards his daughter.

'I don't think you should continue to see that man, Nellie. He is not the right match for you.'

Nellie hated it when her father tried to tell her what to do. She was a grown woman of 21, and perfectly capable of making decisions on her own. 'Actually Father, I do intend to continue seeing him. In fact, Charles has asked me to marry him.'

Anne looked at her father nervously. He was very tolerant of Nellie's stubbornness, but even she knew that this was taking it too far.

'Do you think that is wise, Nellie? You have not known each other for long,' was all her father said, still refusing to turn and look at his daughter.

'He is not from Melbourne Father, but you

know full well he has family connections to nobility in England. I intend to answer yes to his proposal.'

There was silence for a moment. Nellie stared at her father defiantly, waiting for him to oppose her. Instead, he straightened his shoulders and turned calmly towards her.

'Well, it is your decision, Nellie, however foolish.'

Anne stared at her father, unable to believe what she had just heard. Was he going to allow this?

'Nellie is just joking, Father,' Anne said quickly, 'she would never really consider such a marriage.'

'Yes I would!' Nellie cried. 'I am twenty-one years old and it is time I settled down.'

Nellie's father glanced up at her and, for the first time that evening, smiled. 'I doubt you will ever settle down, Nellie, but if this man thinks he can handle you, then I say best of luck to him.'

With that, Nellie's marriage was arranged. Three days before Christmas 1882, Nellie Mitchell became Mrs Charles Armstrong.

The newlyweds honeymooned in Melbourne, giving Nellie a chance to catch up with her old friends, including Pietro Cecchi, who was especially pleased to see her. Nellie loved boasting to them that her new husband had a proper English title – for he was the son of a baronet.

Charles, however, was less impressed with Nellie's friends and excused himself from most of her reunions, particularly when Nellie entertained Cecchi, who Charles disliked the most.

'Are you singing opera in Queensland?' Cecchi asked Nellie during one of their afternoon teas.

'A little,' she replied, 'but I mainly sing popular songs at small gatherings.'

Pietro shook his head. 'That is a waste of your magnificent talent!' he cried.

Nellie tried to pretend that she had little interest in music now, what with her new husband, and a baby already on the way.

Pietro knew her better than that; he knew the life of a jackaroo's wife in the outback would never make Nellie happy.

A month into their honeymoon, Charles got word there was a job for him managing a sugar plantation in Marion, a small town several hundred kilometres outside of Mackay. He was relieved to have a reason to leave Melbourne, and insisted that Nellie get ready to leave as soon as possible.

'Must we return right now? I have barely had time to catch up with any of my old friends,' Nellie replied.

'We have been here for weeks. You have done nothing but see friends,' Charles complained. 'I have to go now. The job won't wait.'

'Well, maybe you should go ahead and get everything ready for me. I could meet you there in a few weeks,' Nellie suggested.

Charles did not like the idea of this, so Nellie eventually agreed to return with him. She said goodbye to her friends, and had a particularly sad farewell for Pietro.

'Are you still interested in having a concert in Melbourne?' Pietro asked her as she prepared to depart.

Nellie looked at him thoughtfully. 'I can't see how that would be possible now,' she said, tearfully.

Pietro kissed her hand. 'One never knows what is possible for a great talent,' he said mysteriously.

A heavily pregnant Nellie thought about Pietro's words throughout the long, uncomfortable train journey to Queensland, but when she arrived in Marion, all thoughts of Melbourne disappeared.

Her years in Mackay had not prepared her for the isolation of her new home. Mackay had had social events, stores and people, but Marion was more like a desert than a town. There was one small shop that functioned as the general store, post office and town meeting hall, but even this was more than 110 kilometres  away from the sugar plantation where she lived in a basic, one-storey house.

Charles tried to make her happy there, but with not even the basic comforts that Nellie had come to expect, she was soon disgruntled and argumentative with him. The one thing she did love about the plantation was the creek where she had to bathe each day, as her house had no bathroom or running water. Bathing in the creek reminded her of her exploits in the Yarra River as a child, and she often took to going down to the creek to bathe and sing operatic arias for hours on end.

Overall, though, Nellie was miserable. Even the Queensland sunshine deserted her so that she had to endure six weeks of constant rain, which left all her beautiful clothes sagging and damp, and her piano mildewed.

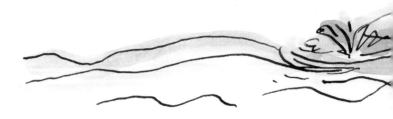

After she gave birth to her son, George, she would take him down to the creek and tell him all about Melbourne and the mighty Yarra and the beautiful men and women who attended the grand opera there. She became more and more homesick, and her relationship with Charles became more unbearable.

'There is a telegram for you,' the postmistress announced one day, as Nellie came into the general store carrying her son on her hip.

When Nellie took the offered envelope, she recognised the writing immediately. It was from Cecchi.

Charles, dusting himself off from the dusty journey into town, walked into the store and started picking out the supplies they had come to gather. Nellie quickly hid the envelope in the bodice of her dress and turned to her husband smiling.

'No post today,' she announced. Charles grunted, intent on choosing some fertiliser on the back shelf of the store.

As soon as they were back at the plantation, Nellie excused herself, telling her husband she was going to the creek to have a bath.

'I am always so filthy after we come back from town. We really should get a covered carriage,' she complained.

At the creek, she settled George down on a rock and eagerly tore open her telegram.

It was indeed from Cecchi, and the contents made her laugh with delight. He told Nellie to come back to Melbourne as soon as she could. It was obvious from the telegram that Cecchi believed she had an admirable talent worth pursuing.

'We have to go back to Melbourne,' Nellie announced at dinner.

Charles looked up. 'Why?'

Nellie showed him Cecchi's telegram. Charles read it, a frown wrinkling his forehead. He placed the letter aside. 'It's not possible, Nellie,' he said simply. 'There is harvesting to do and my contract has several months to run.'

Nellie stared at him silently, making him uncomfortable. Charles finally agreed to stay behind to keep the family business going while Nellie went to Melbourne to pursue her singing.

So, with her husband's reluctant permission, Nellie soon packed her bags, bundled up her son and headed back to Melbourne.

# Chapter Five
# Debut

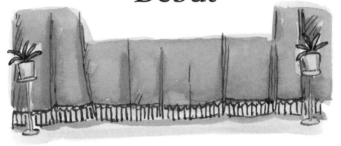

'I don't think I can go on!' Nellie trembled. 'My throat is sore. What if I cannot sing?'

Cecchi patted her hand reassuringly. 'Of course you can. This is the chance you have been waiting for your whole life.'

'But what if I am not any good?'

'You are tremendous. You have the best voice in Melbourne, probably in the world. Once you open your mouth on that stage you will become the most famous singer this country has ever known.'

Nellie tried to control her shaking hands. 'You really think so?'

'Of course. Why do you think I have spent my precious time training you all these years? You are here because of your talent, because of your desire to be a great diva. Do not forget your dream now, not when it is only moments away from being realised.'

Nellie hugged Cecchi and nodded, a look of determination forming on her face.

'Yes, you are right, my dear Pietro, I can't give up now.'

She took a huge breath, steadied herself, then strode confidently out to the stage, her dramatic costume making her look every bit the royalty she was about to become.

As Nellie stepped onstage, there were quiet, murmured whispers and a ruffling of programmes. Her throat seemed to close up as she looked out at all the people in the audience, but then her gaze fell on a distinguished looking man in the third row. It was David Mitchell, Nellie's father. He noticed her gaze and smiled at her, giving her a nod of encouragement. She understood that he was telling her that he was supporting her, he was there for her. Her throat eased and she took another breath and opened her mouth, the beautiful words of Verdi's *Ah! Fors'e lui* flowing from her throat like honey.

There were many other performers on the bill that night, but it was Nellie whom everyone remembered. The young, unknown woman with the impossibly beautiful voice was the talk of Melbourne society for days and was soon booked to sing in the most prestigious opera houses in Australia.

Charles returned from Queensland and, together, Nellie and Charles settled with their son at Nellie's father's house 'Doonside' in Melbourne. Nellie finally had clear reign to pursue her singing dreams.

'Didn't I tell you that you would be the most famous voice in the country?' Cecchi remarked during one of their lessons.

Nellie had been reading a review of her latest performance, which called her 'impressive and powerful'. She tossed the newspaper aside and nodded, taking up a position by the piano, preparing for her vocal exercises.

George sat on the chaise across from his mother, playing with some wooden toys that Cecchi kept for the child to keep him occupied during Nellie's lessons.

'What is wrong, Nellie? Was it not a good review?' Cecchi asked, noticing Nellie's unhappy expression.

'No, no, it was good. They are always good.'

'Then, why so unhappy?'

Nellie shrugged. 'They are always good, but always the same. I have played all the great houses here, everyone has seen me, I have done all I can do in Australia. I feel constrained here.'

Cecchi closed the lid of the piano. 'You wish to go to Europe?'

'Of course I do. To play London and Paris, to sing *La Traviata* in Rome. How can I ever be a truly great singer until I have done such a thing? How I wish we were not so removed from all that great culture.'

'How would you get to Europe, Nellie?'

'I don't know. It is impossible, you are right.'

'You are very famous here, Nellie. In England, France, Italy, you would be a nobody and you would have to start all over again.'

'But you said I have the best voice in the world. Don't you think I could conquer the world stage?'

'I think that we won't have a lesson today,' Cecchi responded. 'You are ready for your performance tonight. Go and enjoy yourself this afternoon.'

Nellie gathered up her things and scooped

up George, smiling at Cecchi. 'Yes, yes, I think you are right.' With that, Nellie sailed out the door.

'How was your lesson today?' Nellie's father asked her in the carriage on the ride home.

'It was fine,' Nellie replied, playing pat-a-cake with George as they headed home to Doonside.

'Do you like Melbourne, Nellie?' her father asked.

'You know I do. Why, what is wrong?'

Nellie looked fearful. She needed her father's financial help if she wished to stay in Melbourne. Charles had no work and although she was singing a great deal, it earned her little money.

'I was wondering if you would not prefer England?' her father asked, keeping his expression neutral.

Nellie's surprised expression was almost enough to make her father lose his composure, but he maintained his stern look.

'England, but how? When?' Nellie couldn't quite grasp what her father was saying. Had her hopes for a chance at a European debut suddenly come true?

'I have been offered the post of commissioner for Victoria to the Indian and Colonial Exhibition in England. I leave for London in three weeks. Charles mentioned that he would be keen to accompany me, so Nellie, I am wondering if you would like to come with us? Your sisters, Bella and Anna, would also be coming, of course, as I cannot leave them in the city unmarried and unaccompanied.'

'You mean it?' Nellie squealed with delight, startling her son and father.

'A little bit of decorum, Nellie, please,' her father chastised.

As Nellie hugged him tightly, her father allowed himself to smile, hugging her back.

After her next performance, she broke the news to Cecchi. 'I was hoping you could write me some letters of recommendation for anyone you know in England and Europe?'

Cecchi stared at her silently.

'I know it is going to be hard for me, Pietro, I do, but can't you see it is perfect? Father has already made all the arrangements. I may sing in the Venice Opera House after all.'

'What about my money?' Cecchi asked flatly.

'What money?'

'You owe me over eighty guineas for singing tuition.'

'But... but you never asked me for any money before?'

'It was agreed you would pay for the lessons once you started to gain payment for your singing. If you leave without paying, I doubt I will ever see this money.'

Nellie couldn't believe her ears. Eighty guineas was a lot of money and she didn't have it. She knew her father would never let her go while there was a debt over her head. Pietro Cecchi, the man whom she had always believed was her biggest supporter had now become the one man who could destroy her dream completely.

Nellie couldn't sleep, worrying about where

she was going to get the money to pay Cecchi. She had less than three days before her ship was due to sail. She could ask her father, but he would be angry and may, in fact, revoke his invitation simply because she was so indebted to Cecchi. Her father had always been unpredictable, and she simply couldn't take the chance.

Sleepless, she thought about all her performances and the people she had met. Whom could she ask for the money?

Suddenly, an idea occurred to her. Her father's brother, Uncle William, would surely loan her the money. He had long been a fan of hers and, like her now departed grandmother, had done all he could to help her realise her dreams of being on the stage. She fell asleep, believing that everything may be okay after all.

'Here's your money,' Nellie spat, throwing

the purse with the eighty-five guineas down on the table in front of Cecchi.

Her old friend was surprised. 'Where did you get this?' he asked, opening the purse and seeing that all the money was accounted for.

'That's none of your business. Let's just say that I have a lot of friends in this city who are happy to help someone with a talent such as mine to reach all the heights allowed to me.' Cecchi blushed. His plan to prevent his star pupil from leaving had seemingly backfired.

'Once I get to London, no doubt I will achieve great fame, Pietro, and when I do, you can be assured I shall make sure that your name is never mentioned in association with mine.'

With that, Nellie strode out of the room and headed towards the docks where her family was waiting for her to board the ship that would take her across the seas to the next chapter of her life.

# Chapter Six
# Europe

London was a huge shock for Nellie. She had always thought Melbourne to be a cosmopolitan city, bustling with life and culture, but compared to London, it seemed like... well, like the small town of Marion. London was full of life, light, people. People were always in a hurry. The city streets were forever bustling, albeit depressingly dark under heavy grey skies, making Nellie feel overwhelmed.

She had a few letters of introduction from friends in Melbourne, including one to the most famous opera composer in London, a man named Arthur Sullivan. Sullivan and his partner W.S. Gilbert were the creators of the most popular comedic operas in Europe, including *The Mikado* and *The Pirates of Penzance.* Just getting to meet him was an incredible opportunity.

Nellie waited in Sullivan's parlour, listening to the trill of other hopefuls in the audition area. She knew her voice was far superior to all those she heard coming from behind the closed door, but still she couldn't help but be nervous, her sore throat returning, as it always did just before a particularly important performance. Sullivan called Nellie's name and she hurried into the audition room.

'What will you sing?' Sullivan asked, not

looking at her as he flexed his fingers over the piano keys.

'I thought *Ah! Fors'e lui* from Verdi's *La Travitore.*'

Nellie began to sing, performing the song beautifully, her voice soaring over the notes.

'Thank you, Mrs Armstrong,' Sullivan interrupted, ending the music abruptly.

Nellie stopped, unsure what to do. 'Was that all right, Mr Sullivan?'

'Yes, yes, fine,' he commented. 'I may have something for you, a small part, perhaps in

*The Mikado* when we revive it next year, if you get a little more training.'

Nellie was speechless. This was worse than outright rejection; the man was offering her a part in the chorus, in a year's time. It was a huge insult to a woman who had never sung any part smaller than the lead.

'Next,' Sullivan called.

Nellie shuffled out, humiliated and angry. London was clearly not going to welcome a singer from the colonies, no matter how talented she may be.

Her other auditions were much the same, with many people flatly refusing to see a woman from Australia, possibly assuming she would be rough and uneducated. A descendent of convicts was not welcome on the stage in aristocratic London.

'I don't care,' she told five-year-old George. 'London was never the great opera city anyway. We are going to Europe.'
Nellie had only one letter of introduction in Europe, for the famed French music tutor Madame Mathilde Marchesi. Getting to Paris would be difficult with no money and with a small child to care for though.

'Please, Father,' she begged, 'it is my last hope to gain any kind of success over here.'
Nellie's father shook his head. He had been supporting her since they had arrived months ago, and although he could well afford it, he certainly did not intend to let

Nellie go outside of his sphere of influence.

'What if I make a deal with you?' Nellie offered.

'What kind of deal?'

'If you give me some money to go to Paris to see Madam, and she refuses to see me, or believes I have no talent, then I will give up on the singing all together. I will enter English society and be the daughter you have always wanted me to be.'

Nellie's father couldn't help but be tempted. There was certainly a part of him that was proud of Nellie's accomplishments and her daring and nerve to pursue success so ruthlessly, just as he always had, but he also knew that the people with which he associated had more than once remarked unfavourably about his daughter's manners and occupation. David Mitchell hoped that Nellie would soon find a way to fit into

English society.

'Okay, Nellie, you have three weeks.'

Nellie's stomach was in knots as she hurried to the address written on her letter of introduction, the apartment of Madam Mathilde Marchesi.

The audition started off like all the others. Nellie watched and waited as several other potential students auditioned for Madam Marchesi, and one after another they were dismissed or given faint praise. Finally, it was Nellie's turn. She steeled herself, preparing for the rejection she was sure she was going to receive.

'What music?' Madam asked in English.

*'Ah! Fors'e lui.'*

Madam nodded, then began to play the piano. Nellie began to sing.

'Why do you screech your top notes?' Madam interrupted. 'Can you not sing softly?'

Tears sprang to Nellie's eyes; she was not good enough. Madam did not like her. Instead of giving up, though, Nellie softened her pitch and continued, allowing her beautiful voice to harmonise with the music.

'Change notes,' Madam ordered. Nellie followed through the range, C, D, E.

Suddenly, Madam jumped up from her chair and disappeared. Nellie stood, devastated as the other girls whispered among themselves.

Madam rushed upstairs to her husband, who was sitting quietly reading the newspaper. 'Salvatore!' she cried. 'I have found a star!'

Madam Marchesi did more than like Nellie's singing, she loved it. She knew talent when she heard it, and was determined to make Nellie her star pupil, whatever it took.

'Your name is horrible, horrible,' Madam told Nellie during one of their lessons. 'You must have a name that will be recognisable throughout the world. You must change it.'

'What should it be?'

Madam shrugged her shoulders, 'Something that says something about you, who you really are.'

Nellie thought for a moment. 'Who I really am is a girl from Melbourne who can't believe she is singing in Paris.'

Madam Marchesi grinned. 'Then that is what you should be called.'

Nellie thought about that. 'Nellie Melbourne?'

'No, no, something pretty. Melba, Nellie Melba. That is who you are.'

In just a few short weeks, under the name Nellie Melba, she was offered a singing contract in Paris for 500 francs per week: a huge amount of money.

Nellie Armstrong, the average middle class girl from Melbourne had become Nellie Melba, a future star of the world stage and one of the most successful singers Australia would ever produce.

# Chapter Seven
## Love

Over the next few years, Nellie conquered audiences throughout Europe. She played huge opera houses and performed in front of the crowned heads of Europe, including Queen Victoria of England and Tsar Nicholas of Russia. She became such a great star that her name was known everywhere, and she was often seen at the best parties and social events.

It was at one of these events that Nellie

met Louis Phillipe, the Duc of Orleans. Louis was a descendant of the last King of France, Louis the XIV, who had been overthrown by the French public during France's fight for democracy almost one hundred years before.

Although France no longer had a royal family, the Duc of Orleans still wielded political influence and was called the 'pretender' to the French throne. A powerful person in France, he was constantly observed, and everything he did made news throughout the country. So when he seemed taken with Nellie Melba, the most famous singer in Europe – and she with him - it was almost impossible for them to keep it a secret.

The Duc of Orleans drew attention to himself by cheering loudly at Nellie's performances, and made no secret of his attraction to her.

Rumours emerged that the two were in love

and having an affair, even though Nellie was still officially married to Charles Armstrong. The public were angry that their 'pretender' to the throne would be so common as to be involved with a married woman, and worse, an Australian!

Nellie and Louis denied the rumours, insisting there was nothing going on between them. They did indeed love each other madly, but Nellie feared that confirmation of their affair would turn the public so strongly against them that her singing career would be destroyed.

No-one really believed their declarations of innocence, particularly Nellie's husband, Charles. The rumours became so strong that news of their affair crossed the channel, and he soon heard of his wife's new admirer.

For years Charles had been unhappy, his life relegated to a mere shadow in the wake of

Nellie's fame. He knew that much of London society thought him a fool, and this latest scandal did little to heighten his position in the vicious social circles he moved in. He still loved Nellie, but he realised that he had to make a stand, and felt forced to speak to the Duc of Orleans.

'Charles, what are you doing here?' Nellie cried.

'I am here to challenge the man who is having an affair with my wife,' Charles announced, striding forward and slapping

Louis across the face with his glove.

Louis jumped up, and Nellie stepped in between the two men. Charles stepped back, rage filling him.

'I want a divorce, Nellie. You have not been my wife for a long time now, and I refuse to be publicly humiliated by you.'

The colour drained from Nellie's face. In 1891, divorce was very uncommon and widely regarded as a terrible sin. She knew that should Charles act on his threat, her affair with Louis would be confirmed and her career would never survive the scandal.

'Please, Charles, calm down. Can we talk about this?'

'There is nothing to talk about.'

Nellie turned to Louis. 'Louis would you mind giving me a few moments alone with Charles, please.'

Louis glared at Charles dangerously. 'If I must,' he said, 'but I am not afraid of this horrid little man.'

Louis walked out of the room as Nellie turned to Charles.

'Charles, please, I know I have been a bad wife to you, and I am sorry for that, but please don't destroy me like this.'

Charles turned away from her, feeling his resolve weakening in the face of her strong personality.

'You have humiliated me, Nellie.'

'I know, but if you divorce me you will destroy my career, everything I have worked for, everything I am. I beg you, please don't do it. I will stop seeing Louis. I will never put your name to shame again.'

Charles shook his head, 'It's too late.'

'Please, Charles, if you ever loved me at all.'

Charles weakened then. 'You promise to stop seeing that French pretender?'

Nellie nodded. 'I promise.'

'All right, Nellie, I won't divorce you.'

Nellie hugged him gratefully. 'Thank you, Charles, thank you.'

'Will you come back to Australia with me?'
Nellie pulled away, surprised. 'No, Charles,
I can't. My career is here. I can't sing in
Australia the way I can in Europe.'

'Singing is the only thing that has ever
really mattered to you, isn't it?' asked Charles.
Nellie nodded, and stepped away from her
husband. 'Yes, that's true. I would do anything
to be able to sing, to be on the stage with my
audience before me. I don't know why, but
it is the only thing in my life that I have ever
truly believed in.'

Charles turned and walked out.

'I'm sorry, Charles,' Nellie whispered, but
he didn't hear her.

Charles kept his promise and did not file for
divorce that year, and Nellie never saw Louis
again. The Duc of Orleans left soon after for
a holiday in Africa, and returned engaged to
a far more suitable match, an Archduchess

from a good European family.

Although Nellie had given up Louis, and had kept her promise not to publicly humiliate Charles, her husband did eventually divorce her in 1900 in Texas. Charles gained custody of their son, George, and Nellie had no choice but to allow Charles to take their son away to America, where she lost contact with them both for several years.

Nellie was heartbroken at having lost contact with George, but women had little power in the legal processes - even a woman as well-known and powerful as Nellie Melba - so, forced to give up her son, she threw herself into her work. She knew the one thing that could make her heart lighter would be to see her beloved Melbourne again, and she insisted on organising an Australian concert tour as soon as possible. She had been trying to return to Australia for years, but the timing had never been right. The seasons in America and Europe meant she could not return to Australia.

Her absence in Australia had been noticed, with members of the Australian press openly suggesting she had abandoned her country.

'How can they write such lies?' Nellie cried, after reading these reports.

'I know, Dear, I know,' Madam Marchesi soothed her. 'You are the most famous thing Australia has ever produced, so as a result they must hate you,' Madame Marchesi grinned, 'but the rest of the world loves you. You should spend your time with us. You have conquered the New World just as you have conquered the old world of Europe. Australia is nothing: a colony.'

It was true that Nellie had conquered Europe and the New World of America, but she was hurt and upset that her true home seemed to hold so little love for her. She wanted the people of Australia to be proud of her.

# Chapter Eight
# A Triumphant Return

In 1902, Nellie organised a tour of Australia, and arrived amid a flurry of activity. The media sang Nellie's praises and Australians turned out en masse to see her.

As Nellie descended the train at Spencer Street railway station in Melbourne, she threw a bouquet of flowers into the crowd, which surged forward, nearly crushing her. Police had to be called in to control the near riot her appearance had sparked.

Since she had been away so long, Nellie insisted that her Australian tour include every state and most major cities of Australia. Nellie was determined to prove she had always loved her country of birth, and wanted every citizen to share in the joy of her return.

The tour was a great success, and Nellie was as happy as she had ever been. Her father, whom she had not seen for years, came to watch her perform in Albury on the border of New South Wales and Victoria. She was shocked at how much he had aged. Gone was the strapping man who had intimidated and inspired her in her youth.

Nellie then took a ferry across the Bass Strait to Tasmania. Unfortunately, there was a storm, and the huge waves and terrifying winds caused Nellie to suffer terrible seasickness. She was so ill that her vomiting caused her throat to bleed, badly damaging her vocal cords.

'You cannot sing, Nellie,' her doctor advised. 'You need to rest your voice for at least three months, or you may damage it forever.'

'But I have concerts booked!' Nellie cried. 'If I don't perform they will believe those horrible reports that I don't care for them.'

'Don't be foolish,' the doctor replied. 'They will understand you are not well. No-one will hold that against you.'

But the Australian media did hold it

against her. When Nellie cancelled the rest of her concert in order to let her throat heal, the press was vicious in its attacks on her, saying that she cancelled the performances not because her voice was damaged, but because she had drunk so much alcohol that she was unable to go on. For years after, Nellie would be labelled a drunkard by the Australian press, something that was as untrue as it was cruel.

The damage to her voice frightened Nellie. The idea she could lose her singing career so easily, her voice lost forever, concerned her greatly. Once before, when she had sung a particularly difficult Wagner Opera, she had damaged her vocal cords, and taking the time off to heal had almost ended her career. She needed to find ways to perform to her demanding schedule without straining her precious voice through overuse.

A year earlier one of Nellie's American friends had told her about a new invention that could record voices and music on wax cylinders and replay them over and over again on transportable records with no loss of quality. Such technology seemed incredible in the 1900's but Nellie had been keen to try it so had agreed that her performance of the song *Allez De Pax* from the *Opera El Cid* could be recorded in this way.

The first recording was done by Lionel Mapleson at the Metropolitan Opera house in 1901 and now Nellie realised that this could be the way ahead in the future.

This new recording technology could save her vocal cords as well as increase her fame and make her voice accessible to those who could not afford the costly expense of coming to one of her concerts.

The record was phenomenally successful when released and soon Nellie was recording and releasing several records per year. By the time of her death she had recorded over 200 records, all of which went on to sell in the millions.

Despite protests from elite opera audiences

that the general public was too stupid to appreciate such high-toned music, it seemed that opera, particularly when sung by Nellie Melba, was a popular form of entertainment for everyone. Through these records, Nellie made her amazing talent available to all who wished to listen, whether a crown head of Europe or a coal miner in Victoria.

Despite her rough treatment at the hands of the Australian press, Nellie still loved her home and was sad that she could not enjoy a career in Melbourne the way she could in Europe. She knew how hard it was for any new Australian singer to gain any kind of opportunity, so she decided to help other aspiring singers by setting up opera and singing classes at the Albert Street Conservatorium of Music in Melbourne, where she established a very generous scholarship for talented young Australians.

In 1909, Nellie returned to Australia with her son George, and bought a house, Coombe Cottage, in the outer suburbs of Lilydale in Melbourne. She had ideas of living in Melbourne for good, but it was still in Europe where the greater opportunities to continue singing existed, and travelling there from Australia took her months by ship. She realised that she still had to live in Europe, but was determined to visit Australia as often as her schedule would allow.

Her visit to Australia in 1914 was particularly difficult, as the war that had been threatening in Europe finally began in earnest. Nellie saw all the brave Australian men signing up to fight for the British Empire in this war, World War I, and decided she must do what she could to help. She realised that her fame could be a powerful tool in gaining much needed money for the war effort, so she immediately began fundraising. Nellie's main charity was the Red Cross, which helped wounded soldiers on the battlefields, but she also supported hospitals and the families of soldiers who were fighting on the western front.

Nellie, knowing how unprepared the sun-loving Australian soldiers would be for the miserable cold of Europe, also decided she would knit socks and jumpers for the men on the frontlines.

Unfortunately, Nellie's domestic skills had never been as good as her singing abilities, and many of her efforts ended up looking rather strange and unwearable.

'I wish I had listened to my mother now!' she remarked. 'She always said I would need sewing skills one day, but I didn't believe her.'

Not one to give up, Nellie organised knitting and sewing groups and paid for all the garments to be sent to the frontlines to warm the soldiers in battle. Still, she knew she could do more, so in 1915, unable to travel to Europe because of the German U-boats patrolling the waters, she boarded a boat for North America and held dozens of fundraising concerts for the war effort, making over 100,000 pounds: a huge sum of money at the time.

In December, Nellie was in Ottowa where the Governor General, the Duke of Connaught, presented her with the Insignia of Lady Grace of St John Jerusalem, in recognition of her services to that order and to the war effort.

The following year, Nellie was required to suspend her fundraising concerts in the US and return to Australia. Her father, who had been ill for some time, had taken a sudden turn for the worse. He died on 25 March 1916, only a few days after Nellie's return.

Nellie had long had a difficult relationship with her father: his strong-mindedness and stubbornness often resulting in conflict between the two. However, she also knew that it was from him that she had gained the strength to follow her ambitions, and that despite his own reservations about her choice of career, he had never stopped loving or supporting his wayward daughter. His death had a profound effect on her and she mourned for several months, unable to resume her fundraising efforts.

The war raged on, and Nellie could no longer ignore her ability to bring comfort and financial assistance to the soldiers and their families. She returned to America in 1917 and, as well as playing big sell-out concerts, organised smaller, accessible concerts at army camps for the newly-trained troops heading to the war in Europe.

Back in Australia, Nellie busied herself organising concerts and fundraising activities. She opened Coombe Cottage for recovering soldiers, held knitting parties and performed throughout the country, raising more money for the Red Cross and other charities.

It never occurred to Nellie to try to capitalise on these efforts for the benefit of her own career, for she truly believed in helping the war effort and supporting the Red Cross. But the British Parliament felt her efforts should be rewarded, so, in 1918, Nellie Melba was made a Dame of the British Empire. This new award had been created to recognise outstanding service to the community by women. Although the award was prestigious, everyone but Nellie herself was told about it.

She had been so busy organising fundraising events that she had not been in Melbourne for the official announcement, and found out by reading it in the papers a few weeks later.

On 2 June 1927, Nellie Melba became the first commoner to receive the newly created Grand Cross of the Order of the British Empire (GBE).

# Chapter Nine
# Retirement

By the end of the war, Nellie had tired of performing. In 1926, she decided to officially retire from the stage, announcing a farewell tour of Australia. There were to be only a handful of performances scheduled, but Nellie had forgotten how much she loved singing, and found it impossible to leave the world of opera behind completely. Her simple farewell tour lasted for more than three years.

She finally retired in 1929, moving into her favourite house, Coombe Cottage in Lilydale, Victoria, where she continued to mentor young singers.

In 1930, Nellie made one last trip to Europe, where she visited all the places that had been so important to her during her early years of success: the Opera House in Brussels where she had made her first truly great European debut; the halls in France where she had practiced with her beloved Madam Marchesi; even the cold, damp rehearsal rooms in London where she had warmed up her voice for her first royal appearance in front of Queen Victoria.

It was a wonderful trip for Nellie as she relived her successes. Often she had to pinch herself to remember how far she had come and how much she had done in her life. Certainly, she had regrets, but she had lived a life few could ever hope for, all because of her immense talent and her drive and determination never to give up.

Nellie sailed back to Australia, but during the trip she developed a blood infection resulting from complications from surgery she had undergone in Europe. When Nellie's boat arrived in Sydney Harbour, she was immediately rushed to St Vincent's Private Hospital in Sydney, where she was under constant medical care. However, there was little the doctors could do.

Dame Nellie Melba died on 23 February 1931, aged 70.

Nellie's casket was first taken to Scots Church, which had been built by her father. After the service, the cortege made its way to Lilydale along a route lined by mourners and spectators. At Lilydale, the casket was transferred to a gun carriage of the Eighth

Artillery Brigade and taken to the cemetery just a short drive from her beloved Coombe Cottage.

Nellie was publicly mourned, and enormous crowds flocked to Melbourne to farewell her. Tributes filled the newspapers around the world, and messages poured in.

Dame Nellie Melba showed the world that Australia could, indeed, produce a star of her calibre. The first true operatic megastar, she led a tradition of success for Australian artists like Joan Sutherland, Kylie Minogue and June Bronhill. Thanks in a great part to Dame Nellie Melba, Australia went from a rural colonial backwater to a country recognised for its talent and culture.

She is still remembered today as Australia's greatest diva, her likeness emblazoned, fittingly, on the $100 note.

# Dame Nellie Melba
# Time Line

*19 May 1861* - *Dame Nellie Melba is born Helen Porter Mitchell in Melbourne, Australia.*

*1867* - *Nellie gives her first public performance at a Richmond school fundraiser when she is barely six years old.*

*1874* – *Nellie is sent to Presbyterian Ladies College, Melbourne.*

*1879* – *Nellie returns home to be with her sick mother.*

*1879* – *Nellie begins singing lessons with retired Italian opera star, Pietro Cecchi.*

*1881 – Nellie's mother, Isabella, dies, followed a few months later by Nellie's four-year-old sister, Vere. Nellie's Father, David Mitchell, moves Nellie and her sister Anne with him to Mackay, North Queensland.*

*1882 – Nellie Porter marries Charles Armstrong and moves to Marion, a small town west of Mackay.*

*1883 – Nellie's only child, George, is born*

*1884 – Nellie returns to Melbourne and has her singing debut to great acclaim.*

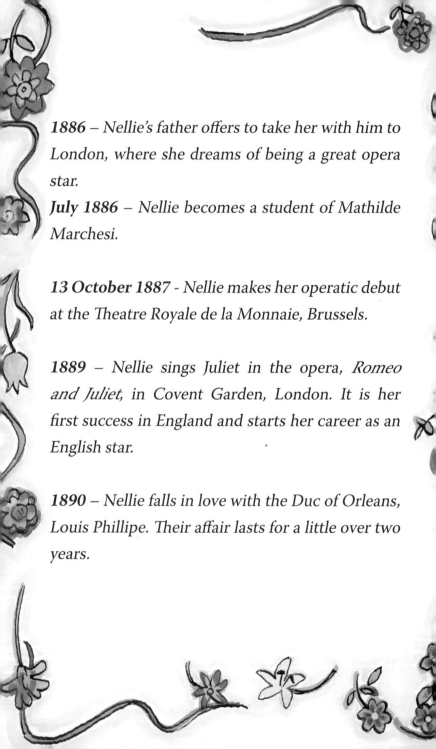

*1886* – Nellie's father offers to take her with him to London, where she dreams of being a great opera star.

**July 1886** – Nellie becomes a student of Mathilde Marchesi.

**13 October 1887** - Nellie makes her operatic debut at the Theatre Royale de la Monnaie, Brussels.

*1889* – Nellie sings Juliet in the opera, *Romeo and Juliet*, in Covent Garden, London. It is her first success in England and starts her career as an English star.

*1890* – Nellie falls in love with the Duc of Orleans, Louis Phillipe. Their affair lasts for a little over two years.

*1896* – Nellie sings Wagner's Opera, Siegfried, and damages her vocal cords, having to leave the stage for three months to recover. It is a rare misjudgment in Nellie's career.

*1900* – Nellie and her husband, Charles Armstrong, are divorced. Charles takes full custody of their son, George.

*1901* – Nellie is the first singer to record her voice using the new voice recording process invented by Thomas Edison in 1877. She sells more than one million records.

*1902* – Nellie embarks on her first tour of Australia. She cancels the tour halfway through, due to damage to her vocal cords caused by sea sickness.

*1909* - Nellie buys Coombe Cottage in Melbourne with plans to settle there. However, her career continues to take her abroad.

*1909* – Nellie returns for a second tour of Australia, singing in almost every town and covering 16,000 kilometres.

*1914* – Nellie is again touring Australia when war is declared in Europe. Nellie works tirelessly for the war effort until 1919, when peace is declared.

*1916* – Nellie's father, David Mitchell dies on 25 March.

*1918* – Nellie is awarded the Order of the British Empire by King George IV of England, officially becoming known as Dame Nellie Melba.

*1927* – Nellie announces her farewell tour and sings the Australian national anthem at the opening of the First Australian Parliament House in Canberra. She is declared Grand Dame of the British Empire.

*1930* – Nellie makes her final trip to Europe.

*1931* – Dame Nellie returns to Sydney and dies from a blood infection. She is moved to Lilydale for burial, where thousands of mourners line the streets to see her last great performance.

Look out for the next title
in the Aussie Heroes series.

SIR EDWARD 'WEARY' DUNLOP

*Aussie Heroes*

Written by Hazel Edwards   Illustrated by Pat Reynolds

Coming soon!

# Aussie Heroes
# Sir Edward 'Weary' Dunlop

Written by Hazel Edwards, Illustrated by Pat Reynolds

Ernie Dunlop was determined to become a doctor. Born in Melbourne, he was fascinated with both medical science and the great outdoors.

Whilst studying medicine he earned the nickname 'Weary' and gained a reputation as a dedicated doctor and sportsman.

In November 1939, after the outbreak of World War II, Weary signed up for the Australian Army. In April 1942 Weary and his men were captured and became prisoners of war. During this time Weary became known for his leadership and communication skills with the enemy.

After the war Weary was committed to caring for war veterans.